Change
in the
Wind

by

Niall OConnor

Thank you Anne
and hope you enjoy the read.

ISBN: 978-0-9576153-0-4

Published by Nobul Publishing
Contact: dublinepost@gmail.com

Printed in Ireland by Gemini International Ltd.

Change
in the
Wind

Acknowledgements

Many of the poems have been previously published by generous editors. I take this opportunity to thank them for their encouragement.

In no particular order, as they are all fine publications!
Outburst
Firstcut
Carty's Journal
Blue Max Review
Revival
Stoney Thursday
Madrush
Corvus
Connotation Press
Poetry Pacific
Galway Review
Revival

Cover by Dave King *Jotunheimar*

All the hard work by Tony Harris, a true friend and without whose skills as a printer, any book would be just be so many loose pages.

And a special thank you to the talented friends who illustrated this book, and to my first wife, Sandra, who has helped illustrate my life . . . so that it is a happy story.

Contents

First Mark	1
Castletownshend	2
Monument unfinished	3
Fairy Tales	4
Mumbo Jumbo	4
Removing the Ivy	5
Walled Garden	6
Rock	7
Stand Back!	8
Outsider	9
Poets at Tara	10
The Pub Cat	11
Tea Leaves	12
The Poet	13
Climbing Mount Kilimanjaro	14
New Angles	16
An Impossible Event	17
First Time	17
Tethered	18
Child of mine	19
The Name	20
Abraham's Altar	21
The Japans	22
East West	23
The Clothes Line	24
Crete	25
Dance	26
Dancing at the Crossroads	27
Fermoy	29
Eye	30
EArTh	30
The Ironic Age	31
Gathering the Kindling	32
The City	33
The Halfpenny Bridge	34

Wild Geese 35
Revolution 36
Collateral 37
A Full Tank 42
Molassey Cottage 43
The Sea 45
The River 46
Change in the Wind 47
Dingle Peninsula 49
Ballyferriter 50
The Weather Forecast 51
Writing Poetry 52
After the Funeral 53
Venetian Downpour 54
Autumn 56
Ode 57
Prometheus Bound 58
Moon 58
The Fire 59
Sleeping Woman 60
Budapest 61
Emily 62
Jeremiah B 63
Remembering 64
Roots 65
Snow Girl 68
The Banal 70
The Homecoming 71
P. J. Birmingham 72
Important Historical Events 73
Snow 74
Trees 75
The Final Concert 76

First Mark

With this first mark,
I make a path — stepping stone words
through an otherwise empty space.

with this repetition, I strengthen,
widening the space,
invite others to follow

now that the path has been drawn,
— the questions. Why here? Why now?

each new poem exploring
this wondrous garden,
where we weeds have grown.

Castletownshend

Formula one bees and wasps
criss-cross overhead,
and I lie beached in a welcome backwater
on a rock that generations
have both cursed and blessed;
near where the wild land meets the sea
and crow and seagull do war
for the pickings, from both tip and shore.

The put-put-putting to sea of the one-man fishing boat
stitches peace and permanence,
as they go out to examine patient lobster pots,
baited and waiting.

Lobster or cuckold,
both strained from the sea by deceit,
whoever has enjoyed
the last supper, now takes his turn
to be enjoyed.
There is no guilt in sacrifice
here.

Monument unfinished

nine stones I piled up
each plucked from the Atlantic rage
nine images I shaped
of a life segmented by age
and into a tower they tottered
tongue-tied and eloquent
a monument writhing
on a boulder millennia old
nine stories till then untold.

Angela Cox

Fairy Tales

All fairy tales are loaded with dread
Evil witches and trolls
Around the young child's bed.
Adult titillation at nature's cruel breast;
Twisted symbol,
Passed through without test.
One to titillate, one to scare
One for the daydream
One for the dare.

Mumbo Jumbo

Looking for the lowly humbug
mumbo, jumbo
elephant ideas
in an airy, fairy
not quite so scary, circus
ring, ring
sing
of nonsense rhymes
mimes
inconsequential probabilities
paradoxical walls
fall.

Sebastian

4

Removing the Ivy

We crunched our way
across the frozen meadow
two robots, over wrapped
against the cold.
Surrounded by silent sleeping trees
and steamy breath, we plucked and picked
at the frozen ivy,
teasing its tentacles
from the dark, and cold Roscommon stone.

Our aunt had told us
that we would save the wall,
save it from the fate of older families
who had lived nearby, in now
humbled heaps of drawing rooms and kitchens
upstairs, downstairs, all a-jumble
piles of random dice, tossed aside
each settling a new insult, a new revelation.
Families bound by servitude and obligation.

Our white and pink child fingers,
like lepers at scabs,
worked until our breath
no longer steamed, and we stole away
to hide, in the warm stables nearby
where oppressed donkey-companions
observed our shivering bodies
with smug disdain.

Walled Garden

Great garden walls
echo the voices of children within,
and bamboo jungles scrape the sky
above my outstretched schoolboy limbs.

I search beneath the mesh of sound,
gurgling water, flittered song
to find a silence that will bind
the meaning, I glean beneath the weave.

Winds that pass through purple grasses
mimic the voices of playing children,
but inside the rhododendron den I still wait;
crouched inspector of this adult state.

Rock

A rock . . .
well really the brow of a rock . . .
its heart lay deep and hidden,
but when I lay my cheek against it
in the heat of the summer it cooled
and I could feel the great primeval thump of its heart
comforting me, when nothing else was understood.
I clutched this great rock,
my only constant in a life of changes,
while the earth itself, with me holding on tight,
flew at increasingly careless speeds
through my teenage years.

Beneath the arched viaduct it squatted
uncomplaining of the shafts of steel
driven deep, and the weight of the stone it carried;
my teenage weight, of little importance.
It was always there when I came,
in dream or even in reality
taking the time to be calm and listen
as I told it of my hurts and confusions.

One summer, I foreswore all others
and promised it my heart
if it would only turn it to stone,
but though Rock listened
I knew its answer without it having to speak
I was being selfish
and it would have given all of its great strength
to feel,
just a little, of my pain.

Stand Back!

Stand back
and let the dog see
the rabbit, he cried
let the urge take hold
and the chase begin.

I thrash against my binds,
fears imagined . . . and real,
scratch furiously with pen,
scrambling to get not just anywhere,
striving to remain absolutely still.

But the rabbit has bolted,
disappeared back into
the warren that is my mind;
each memory
another twist,
each love a turn.

Outsider

Introverted, green clad walls,
surround the old monastic site;
peaceful in passing,
but de facto prior industrial age,
now tightly fisted,
by the squireens and thought brokers.

We bent the knee or left.

Each morning the rusted bus
with its fading plimsoll line
ferried its cargo to the nearby city
where we dreamt, and planned the great escape;
each isolated in his own cocoon,
fearful of the label,
proud of the slogan:

Outsider

Scott Anthony Kelly

Poets at Tara
- the High Priest, The Corner boy, and the Court Jester

We came to the Hill of Dreams
to hide out in a church yard
and listen to dreamers
showcase the magic they had weaved
from themselves, for us.

We must have been a strange sight there
amongst the headstones and ancient wood
for the crows periodically broke into
raucous laughter at our bumbling attempts
to make ourselves understood.

The words of Heaney, Muldoon and others swirled
bravely above the graves, but none could release
me from the cold embrace, of the damp that rose
from the corpse rich earth below.

I scanned the distance for an understanding
of what my part in all this was, and
after words we walk from the Hill in silence
trailing the last of the moment and feelings, down
to the roadside where commerce began.

There I covered
and watching from a doorway
I saw the chit-chatting progress
of my fellow travelers and quietly putting away
their thoughts like half eaten sandwiches
in a picnic basket.

The Pub Cat

It was the feline that gave me status
permission to listen, analyse.
I sat by the fire in the country pub;
cat napping. If the house pet
would use my lap to sleep
then they too would bide my presence.

They came from small farms
of handkerchief fields, and told their stories;
each shared memory safe and familiar
in its retelling,
tribal feelings of self reservation
disarmed temporarily.

I drank from their well
as thirstily as any parched man might do
The cat purred content with his new lap
and the stroking I gave,
and was smug in the knowledge
that I as stranger,
couldn't say shoo!

Angela Cox

11

Tea Leaves

A sunset fills the bottom of my porcelain cup,
born between thought filled hands,
transparent from the fierce breath of a kiln
whose sole purpose was to destroy or immortalise.

When they have settled,
and the evening sky is clouded,
the leaves gather gossiping
to tell their final tale.

So I tip the cup upside down,
and turn it once, twice, three times,
all the time chanting the tinker woman's chant,
willing one future to reveal.

But when I clutch the base one last time,
I am unwilling to see,
and quickly turn to the tap instead
and scatter runes like stars
to the sink below.

Each leaf in falling takes its own path,
all leaves spiral home.

The Poet

He types
staccato of self-determination
Control
punctuating the bubble of his environment with
Decoration
until
a swirling prismatic light splinter is
thrown at random from his child's
Pencilled lips.

Climbing Mount Kilimanjaro

The garden zone -friendly, then the forest zone -cool.
Night fell too soon, the steeply sloped rain forest and
the servant hills, slipped underneath us, in the dark.

I fought my way up, headlamp illuminating
nothing but poring dirt; all around me the sounds
of leopards, snakes; geography confused, in this
primordial forest, where life springs from decay.

We camped, and stripped to nakedness, trying
to rebuild our shattered spirits with folded clothes
and tea. Sleep came uninvited, like a burglar
silently stealing half finished cups from sudden
limp arms.

Next morning, saw the departure of those who could
take no more of this risk route; trip turned to hard task;
each day, life thinning out, nothing left to be shared,
but pollo, pollo, slowly,slowly.

And then we left the earth, there could be no rescue,
. . . even helicopters need air to fly.
On we climbed, and lungs breathed normally,
but our tired muscles never received relief,
and not a sound, other than those you made your self,
not even an echo, to keep an empty skull company,

We were now beyond the zone of life.
Beneath us, the jets like pond skaters
criss-crossing the pond that was Africa,
and the curve of the world lay below
and beyond.

On the last night, we tricked the mountain
using its frozen shale to climb when she slept.

By the time the sun had risen, we had reached her
top, standing ragged for our moments glory each
a god among men, albeit with feet of clay.

Descent was by the coca cola route,
and with each thousand metres we fell,
fresh tears came, as emotion
and life, and oxygen returned.

I called your name to save me,
but even my footsteps . . .
you had already erased.

New Angles

I
like
to write
poems in triangles

but most of my good
friends use rectangles

so I thought that
today I would
find a
new
way, to inveigle
first prize from new angles

An Impossible Event

This is the impossible event horizon
and these words, the impossible event

Why do I think I can paint pictures
on the canvas of another's mind

Mix the real and the imagined,
in a suspension of shared humanity

Trust this will allow me
the briefest of connections

Validation of a single existence;
from the hive mind disconnected.

First Time

In a grubby city centre flat,
on sheets impregnated with
lives that would never be,
she came on condition
that it would not mean anything;
so I being selfish, to this agreed.

Years later, I discovered
she took part of me away, surreptitiously,
and I search for what I did not know
in a small body, that I still remember
without curves,
though it insinuates itself
into each and every dream.

She stole, what I had not yet to give
but wanted all the same.

Tethered

Soles of feet now more tactile
than translucent fingers
fumbling feelings
each blade of grass,
each worm cast caul
even the grey grass mantled rocks
warming their backs in the sun
are an emotional chiaroscuro.

Inside, a manatee does somersaults
and all reality is changed.
I am accepted.
I have accepted.
I am a vessel for creation
and am tethered once more;
the transposed umbilicus,
completes the circle.

Elida Maiques

Child of mine

You are the hard pressed slippery bundle,
heterotrophic,
that forced tears of happiness,
equally hard borne from my eyes.

You were the teacher of love
with your first breath,
and the eyes of trust and belief
with all your growing, and now
you are the tabernacle of my existence,
diminished only by me;
custodian of both our dreams,
keeper of the secret
that has already passed,
and lies within you.

Peace and Love.

You are the child I trust,
to always be yourself.

With each thought and breath you grow,
strange intimacy of life
that this makes us strangers.

You were in my first breath,
and I will be in your last.

The Name

The neighbours had a collection;
consolate solidarity,
and the cardboard box, bars the living
room amid photographs that look
anywhere but there.

A purple scarf, bruise coloured,
hides the mark of shame.
Dare I speak her name?

Friends ornament her coffin,
now a play-box
with butterflies and birds,
and messages of good intention,
no intervention.

Her pretence is so perfect,
for a moment I forget
images of hanging grub;
images of transformation
deformation.

Memorialised objects and tokens litter
below rosary beads she never held;
red shoes are pretty,
soles dust-free.
Can I delete her now, from my phone?

After the house is organised,
decades of the rosary are impressed.
For the collective
there is nothing else
left to do.

With pale lips held tight,
she whispers:
you would not understand.
Now I know I never will.

Abraham's Altar

Cold stone
wrenched
from the warm womb of mother earth
forms a memory crypt,
and stale incensual memories
lie heavy, and hormonal
over the white, wax-stained, sheet
that covers Abraham's altar.

Saintly downcast eyes
- alabaster surveillance-
watch the comings and goings,
as salvation is dolled out by incantation
and holy water.
Lives blessed in, and out.
Tears shed carelessly by anointed hand.

The Japans

On the eleventh day of March
two thousand and eleven
the tether is broken, and
a long suffering beast

breaks free for an instant,
searching for the open seas
like Brendan's sleeping whale,
prompted into movement

by a nuclear harpoon
set alight on its back
from langorous resting place
this sleeping giant disturbed.

One month later the cherry
blossom halleluiahs
in riotous praise of life;
an iridescent echo

of the sprouting ginko trees
disdaining the erasure
of Hiroshima.
Then, the echo like thunder

rolls to my small back garden
in Dublin, where a cherry tree
splays a choir of gaping pink
and also heralds resurrection.

East West

I sit in an Indian restaurant
sheltering from the wet embrace of a Dublin summer's day
served by the three great book religions,
and mediate my place in this great scheme.

Through the looking glass of a rain
blistered window
the nation flags frantically direct
winds to east and west.
and a crow with imperial aspirations
sits atop,
veering neither way.

Not one recognises his declaration,
and so with an imperial toss of his black cloak
he casts himself away,
leaves the flags to their feverish sorting.

The Clothes Line

We meet over the folding of sheets, dividing
halves carefully into halves,
until we yield one.

Then the family semaphore signals a new
arrival, and bras play openly in the wind
with long john's that dance a merry tune, beside
baby's jump suits; playthings
that invite no more comment than a smile.

But now the line is empty,
lies coiled, still tethered
to its knotted start,
poised to spear loneliness,
into any passing, unguarded heart.

Crete

The insect screech, circadian
signals again, the dominance
of heated sun, over land and man

lines of olive trees cling
to the shoulders of heroes old
gnarled, twisted trunks that tether

the restless silver shoals constantly
turning beneath the midday sun,
old wood pushing young whips

to drip green stoned fruit
on generations, that have served loyally
the gods of land, and sea, and sun;
man's ingenuity and nature's graceful guile
as one.

Dance

Dance is Life he told me,
forked rivulets springing,
from august temples.
Springs of eternal youth,
still willing his efforts forward.

They had danced from Budapest in '56
out of necessity, — the Csàrdàs their only passport,
and each evening, with a new cry for freedom,
they performed, after the dancing bears
and the Gypsy fiddler.

From Vienna to Paris,
Rome to Amsterdam, a dancing troupe
that carried their country in carpet bags
and hidden in the tips and heels
of their shared heartbeat.

Dance is Life he told me
in a low ceilinged, basement restaurant,
that had not seen a summer,
or winter, for at least four hundred years,
and his woman stroked the back of his cupped,
resting hand, that still reminded her
of the arched back, and its challenge.

She hides modestly now
behind the vase of plastic flowers
she soothes the friss of his heart in affirmation
of a time when he released,
and caught her again, at will,
   . . . forever in his orbit
tripping over heartbeats with each approach.

Dancing at the Crossroads

On the old coach road,
between Ballyjamesduff and Cavan town,
there is the village of Crosskeys.

Pubs three, residents four, and a road that runs through it
crossed by another, that rises from the village green
to the nearest hill where the church was built, to be seen.

On the other side, the same road falls
through a passage in the drumlins,
until it gets lost in the black earth fields,
terminating in a rusted gate
as all great roads ultimately do.

That is all there is; a remnant of a village
once a mill, and a thriving barracks,
the village is now just a curiosity item;
a jigsaw picture added, piece by piece,
each time you drive quickly through.

We stopped there one day, late in the summer,
when in the country, all is either saved or lost;
harangued by posters at every turn on the approaching roads,
we stopped to investigate the Crosskeys Harvest Festival.

First we walked the green, and discovered a small stream,
with pansies and closely cropped grass,
and a juvenile River Erne once set to work at the mill,
in a time when the young were always for hire, for a pittance.

Then the sun scuttled quickly behind the clouds,
its work of introduction completed,
and we were ushered to the pub by a dark squall,
and the threat of rain.
Inside, the lights were turned up,

and a small timbered dance floor
was separated from the dark,
and while I supped, with rising anticipation.
a women passed in, long ski bag under arm,
and quickly erected a polished pole
of stainless steel, ratcheted expertly
between ceiling and floor.

Two youths came then, and ordered cokes,
sat whispering excitedly behind cupped and sweaty palms,
while local women appeared from doors and dark
to dance the pole, just for the lark.

Fermoy

When I return
I see myself as stranger
in that town of forty winters,
and summers past;
walk awkwardly, uncomfortable,
a time traveller fearing
the paradox of meeting
himself.

Everything and nothing has changed,
just like the constant rate of the river flow,
thunderous beneath the promise
of leaping salmon throwing themselves
against time's weir.

Aliens look strangely familiar,
and I try to read the DNA riddles
written on their cryptic faces,
guilt ridden when caught in study.

Dismissive they are,
since I look past them to see others
and everything seems to be as it was
except the grave of my mother
and father
who I have now come
to meet in years;
true siblings
left behind.

Eye

Eye is
organic
watching itself in the mirror, panic
constant refocus and sibling resistance
reluctant concession
of each other's
Existence.

Eyeball - not crystal ball
murky
sight bound by maternal tomb
in every black holed iris
a galaxy's womb

EArTh

We have tested and tasted
all that earth has to offer:
heterotrophic mankind
consumer of all life forms
including ourselves.

Now we set out
peaceful and curious
on a voyage of discovery
to the rest of the universe.

What do you - the as yet uneaten –
think about that?

The Ironic Age

the Ironic age is manmade, I say
and we are in an age of plenty
where everything is measured,
Four
and so everything can be managed.

the 'bags of mostly water'
walk the surface of the moon,
and our ambassador-drones scour planets
Eight
for life forms, that we have not already eaten.

earth is being terraformed in rehearsal
for the next candidate earth, and everybody is a poet
or a banker - or both.
Twelve
the world is now a village.

husband messages wife via satellite,
'home sn jst arnd krnr'
tonight I ate kiwi from New Zealand, beans from Kenya, and
Sixteen
a nice little sorbet, that was made under licence in Holland
for a German company . . . how cool is that!
twenty.

twenty people, just like you, and me
have died of hunger
when you read this poem . . .
could you not have read
just a little bit faster?

Gathering the Kindling

After the shifting spring storms
beneath the sleeping branches
a mother gathers kindling

to maintain an ancient fire.
Two children trail, and a third
lies wrapped on wheels. All in pink

they dutifully mimic
the gathering, heaping their
sticks into a tangled pyre

unconsciously passing
this ancient test. The mother
gathers left-handed, fingers

varnished stiff, and scissored
about smoking cigarette,
cursive body in worn blue

denim. Deceived, she forgets
their task and plays, roles shifting
from harvesting to the hunt

and each hides in turn behind
the unmoved trees, and awaits
discovery, and the threat

to continued survival
here, where lives like dried sticks
are gathered up, from beneath
the blossom trampling feet.

The City

Tall trees stand
as organic tributes to a bucolic passing

bovine sculptures in a concrete age.
Steel car-pods shuttle

sub-routines of a wired world,
and wailing sirens demand attention
like spoilt brats in a mad kindergarten.

This is the city where
all heads turn in expectation

towards any bloodied scene unfolding,
where the individuals theory of immortality

is never discredited, in one's own lifetime.
Constantly we are nurtured by self medication

the act of creation and recreation.
The city, just a tottering pile of coloured bricks
in the hands of a self-centered child.

The Halfpenny Bridge

Georgian iron and treacherous timbers,
slime covered and slippery
up and down;
a pox on the ferryman's earnings
by those who dare to cross
from mean street to Venetian passage,
this is the Ha'penny bridge

Leaning on both North and South,
owned by neither, both,
a no-man's land
twixt Norse and Brit,
chained to the granite quays.

On its crest,
its pinnacle,
the luckless Lord Mayor of Dublin;
the toll gatherer-beggar,
with his bowl forever sits,
selling poverty for a pittance,
and redemption for avoiding eyes

The royal barge,
the chieftains byre,
bananas from Bolivia,
they all have passed
beneath this throne,
this crown of Anna Livia.

Wild Geese

Irish youths sit in Cretan restaurants
and arms that once guided a plough
or sleán or spade,
now drape ornamental, back of chair

no work stained collar, nor waistcoat, nor
shiny fumbled, grease, knotty . . .
no cloth cap
to top their youthful confidence;
plucked from the soil but
still displaying its mark
despite the practiced indolence

hands that wait the training tether
and tilted heads that listen
weather vane
for cheek-felt wind, eyes narrowed
in shrewd calculation,
straightened leg careless thrown

all things that show
these minds have yet to know a place
which is not green, and sharpened by
wild eyed whiskey talk.

Revolution

There is talk of revolution everywhere
from mouths that have never
used the word before,
except maybe to talk about
the poor broken countries,
-banana republics-
just like ours.

Will green fields be returned to grass?
Will towers raised high for increased yield
be leveled and returned to field?

Now the babies that were sent to creche
will stay at home, with mum and dad,
and grannies man the checkpoints
and granddads set up
window cleaning routes.

What new statues rise
when old icons fall?

Collateral

(The words in italics are taken
from a U.S. Operational Video Recording.
The observers are you and me.)

July 12, 2007

The 30mm cannon fire left about
a dozen people dead
two children, two journalists: all insurgent.
some were armed, but all now
appear to be relaxed.

before the cannon shell rained down
the ten were largely unknown,
fathers and sons, lovers and husbands.
the two were known as Saeed and Namir,
a journalist and a cameraman.
the children are still unknown
    . . . for their own protection.

there is no question
that coalition forces, were
clearly engaged in combat operations
. . . against a hostile force,
the Lieutenant-Colonel said, and
all was in accordance with
the rules of armed conflict, and the rules
of engagement. The operation was videoed
encrypted, buried, then released again
    . . . illegally

but wait, there is more.
they keep walking, and
one of them has a weapon?
a camera examines a camera

and does not recognise itself;
the man decides.

Yeah Roger. I estimate
There's probably about twenty
Oh yeah . . .
Hey Bushmaster element
Copy on the one-six
That's a weapon . . . Yeah
Hotel two six: crazy horse one eight
Fucking prick
Have individuals with weapons
Have five to six individuals
With AK 47's
Request permission to engage

the cross marked a centre on dust cloud
and men scattered
protecting their heads from 30mm cannon
with knuckles of bone as white as bleached skull.
seven fell, one ran drunkenly;
an out runner searching for base,
a cameraman
being searched for the best shot

Keep shootn', keep shootn'

Saeed touches base against the shattered rubble

Keep shootin'

the cross searches him out, pokes him, then
it interrupts a spasm with one final punch
nothing but silence and dust now, and smoke.

Roger, I got 'em
Oops I'm sorry
God damn it Kyle
All right hahaha I hit 'em
Bushmaster six this is bushmaster two six
Got a bunch of bodies layin' here
Yeah we got one crawling around down there
But, uh you now, we definitely got something.
We're shooting some more
Roger

the already deceased individuals got on with their dying:
they do not respond
rising spirits of dust erase the scene
the only protection is illusion
so Saeed lies still

Hotel two six you need to move
To that location when Crazy Horse is done
And get pictures, over
Six beacon Gaia
Oh, yeah, look at those dead bastards
Nice

the black and white images
now have black stains that frame
Those dead bastards . . . .nice!
crosshairs admire their handiwork
looking for upright lines to lock onto;
there are none.
brick and body parts are jumbled,
crazy horse circles, circles

There's one guy moving down there
But he is wounded
He appears to be trying to crawl away

Saeed lifts one knee, one head.
a floundering body makes no sense

He's getting up
Maybe he has a weapon in his hand
I'll put two rounds near him
Yeah roger that

Saeed, legs in gutter, blood draining neatly away
pushes towards an open gate . . . sanctuary
legs, and left side do not respond.
still . . . in . . .   gutter.

Come on buddy
All you gotta do is pick up a weapon
Bushmaster six this is bushmaster two six
Yeah bushmaster we have a van
That is approaching and picking up the bodies
 Ok yeah
We have individuals going to the scene
Looks like . . . possibly . . . picking up weapons and uh
bodies
Let me engage

two children look up at the distant helicopter,
two men run to check Saeed,
help has arrived.
the adults are silent,
but the children have seen this all before,
so they watch the whirly bird and wonder
will it drop food, or messages, or death?

Crazy-horse Eighteen, permission to engage

Dada says stay in the van.

Come on let us shoot! Come on!

the Cross hovers hungrily
on Dada's jellabiya,
he is trying to straighten Saeed

Bushmaster crazyhorse One eight
They're taking him. Roger.
We've got a black SU . . . uh bongo truck
Request permission to engage.

the van shudders, the dust explodes
the shells rip from ceiling to road
Dada says stay in the van.

Clear!

the van's roof is unstitched

Clear!

dust and smoke obliterates, and
the Crusader's cross hovers once more,
frustrated and forever seeking, seeking,
solidity lost, it is unable to deliver
its final blessing

Clear!

Crazy Horse is just a helicopter, and
its brain is made in neutral Ireland.
all the hard bits that really hurt
are stamped: Made in the USA,
with Chinese steel.
The Cross is used to focus.

A Full Tank

For days, then weeks
running into years
I shuttled to and from work,
slowly weaving a web of habit
that constrained by mind,
continued my dire existence.

Then one day, I set out
to a job that was there no longer,
and I saw a tank full of petrol,
that would not be used in dribs and drabs;
a tank of two hundred miles or more
that I would use . . .
use it all . . . in one unrationed day.

So I drove.
I drove west, racing ahead of the morning sun
imaging myself as the herald of a new day,
every arrival a new beginning
and when I reached the sea I stopped
and was amazed to find it was still there
where it has always been,
waiting without complaint for my return,
waiting within for its time to rise.

Molassey Cottage

We were here, when the swallows had come,
to prepare their young
for the long flight south,
to the waterholes of Africa.

You may be here, when they return again,
or even when the first flutters of snow will fall
past the foraging grey squirrels
where the hazel stands tall.

And because you're tired, you may come
to draw from a memory of quieter times,
or share with your impatient and restless young
the peace that can be found in simpler rhymes.

But whenever, and whatever, draws you near,
you will know that when here you dwell,
from the trees there will coo a lullaby
and its woodland waters will weave a spell.

Angela Cox

The Sea

And the river feeds
the vast insatiable hunger of the sea
where it meets the land,
and me

and men place stones
that were born elsewhere from fire
to enclose this birthing place
of land and soul
. . . dark wall of granite
bearded, worn

and the sea reaches out
for the sky she meets but cannot touch;
by the shore for which she
yearns so much
rebuffed

and my soul stretches out
from where I stand, in conjoined silence
with the lonely swell
waiting

for I am drawn to where the sea
heaves itself against the sky,
and the limits of a small man's
expansiveness
and I am the petrel on wings of foam
grazing the swelling, hypnotic depths,
for what the deep discards.

The River

I owned a river once
and it owned me
we walked together, mind and spirit,
and it set my childhood free.

I loved a river once
and it loved me
neither eddy nor current
concealed any mystery.

I once hit that river
beat its back with a stick
but then I cried for my river
and it cried for me.

When I wept over its waters
it mixed its tears with mine
Flow gently sweet river
'till the ends of time.

When I walked with my river
it seemed to dally for me,
surely now it will take my ashes
all the way to the sea.

Change in the Wind

It was a long summer of lean bodies
and their learning.

We took a boat from beside the pier and pushed off
into the wide —my brother and me—
heading out through the tide filled bay
for the open sea, and the mackerel
we dreamed of catching there
with our lines of rainbow feathers,
and our boys' imagination.

I oared first, and then when tired,
passed them over, and lay sheltered
between the twisting gunnels;
admiral and high lord of the seas

after a distance, the influence of the land was fading,
and the tide turned,
and because the sea and sky are closely wedded,
the skies darkened, and the winds blew persistently
from the land, driving us further and further,
into their hungry embrace

regaining the oars
I drove down with concentration
and the effort and desperate rhythm, of a man
trying to hurry in the dark before his worst fear

to the right of me, my compass point;
a craggy outcrop of blackened rock
stayed in the distance, persistent,
and I could not gain because of wind and strain
from racing tide

three times I almost slumped, hands raw, mind rent,
back strained at every draw; wing dips of faith
into an alien and monstrous world

and then, just as suddenly
we found the shelter of the land,
and with the sky lifting its weight,
we were allowed through
and the sounds of the small grazing rush of our hull,
and my dipping oars, took us all the way home.

Dingle Peninsula

down from the rising altar stone of
Binnn Diarmada,
na Gorta Dubha spread below
through the reed beds we go
to the wiry dune grass
where the bones that have travelled
make the beach white, the mind wide,
bodies who sought sanctuary from the storm,
delivered cold and sightless
given back when the waves tired
of their playthings

montbretia clinging to stone walls,
keeping its nobbly toes dry
wears a headdress, of closely cropped briars
black-beaded with the taste of summer
glorious in the autumn sun;
a larder of winter food and shelter,
a place behind which you might heap up a new field,
for a future generation.

I find the fellowship, of myself here
and all who have gone before me.
in this holy, West of Dingle peninsula
I find the same landscape
is cradle and grave,
knows the brooding, and the gathering,
the harvest, and the beach comb,
the storm, and its aftermath.

Lives like candle flames
shelter behind stone walls
from the onslaught;
each man rediscovers his own cave,
where he is companion to himself,
and all he can carry.

Ballyferriter

each little house with a world of its own
safely tucked beneath a grey shell
for a generation, or two

and when the sea is full
it calms
content to nestle up against
the warm heart of a supine earth
a surface for living laid down
by hard men with gentle souls,
the cloak of Brigid
over this land of rock and sea

and always the wind
and what it carries
blowing from beyond the edge
of the earth,
out there where the sun goes each evening

hardening into a flattened disc before slipping down
into the otherworld
out there where the holy ones sent their
sacrifice and prayer
and against whose threat
kings erected ramparts of stone
that have since been overthrown
by science and new beliefs.

Now we face east.
east to await the risen Christ,
east to the bigger island,
east to the Empire of Europe,
and still the wind and what it carries
comes from over the edge of the earth,
bringing the first breath . . . and its promise.

The Weather Forecast

Wind for the lamb
rain for the calf
sun for the foal,
and if you can hang
your hat and coat on the moon,
its sure sign of the bad weather to come.

Mare's tails and mackerel scales
make tall ships take in their sails
and rainbow in the morning
gives you fair warning

but there is always surprise
when a rainbow springs up,
and between dusk and dawn,
not a single heartbeat is missed.

Writing Poetry

Old fumbled feelings
remain coiled with vicious potentiality
in the dark cave that is my mind
unsatiated, unresolved.

Thoughts are cast aside
like tide-worried stones,
rounded from the comings and goings
relentless polishing of everything between.

Bone beaches of words
remain as runes of mind, and
I continue to send out the invitations
to those who have been uneasy bed companions
elsewhere

Please come and sit together
at my wedding feast.
Seating arrangements however
are difficult, and rarely final.

After the Funeral

After the funeral we gather
four full-bodied men
once a clutch of speckled purpose
now dulled and awkward with grief.

We toe the line that is the parents' death
and notice with embarrassment
the scuffed toe cap
side by side
with the brand new shoe.

This is a time for disentanglement
and each drawer is trawled
each picture scanned
for memories that can be shared.

We look for clues as
to why an object was cherished
so long, — why an after image
can represent a life.

In the attic I find my treasure tin:
a horse made of clip-clops
a ball of stringed ideas
a soldier stiff backed and with no fear
a car of squeals and vrooms
the forgotten pet beetle now hollow
the conker with a chestnut tree still inside
the butterfly painter of meadow's flowers — pinned
and the skipping stone, still waiting for its next attempt.

continued . .

All these things that held my life suspended
since the lid was last pressed down
now have the awkwardness and distance,
of an overheard conversation
between estranged lovers.
Time changes all.

Venetian Downpour

This is a city that stands on its own reflection
its people hidden behind darkened doorway
and redbrick walls,
walls marked with the plimsol line of history
and tides;
the ebb and flow of trade,
and the resolve of man and his stubbornness
to place a city
where it is not wanted,
triumphant columns rampant,
mirrored in each square by wells, leading
to the fresh water trapped below.

I wander the meandering streets;
always beside, and over the greeny
blue salt waters of the open lagoon
in an act of faith . . . or folly

In St Mark's Square the pigeons strut,
ready for instant coupled flight,
while I sit impaled, feet fixed
to floats of stone, imagining
what it is to soar.

continued

On the Rialto Bridge,
masks to cover the poxed and the beauty,
and sounds all round sharpened by the clink
of cutlery on glaze, and murmurs,
conversation over latticed chairs
awaiting the impending downpour.

High up between the roofs of the tiled
and the terraced, grey titan clouds
prepare to shed themselves and a chill
descends before the sky and the sea
are united in one furious
female deluge.

Autumn

Match day crowds of fallen angels
gather against the red brick lines
built with trapped bubble and twines
congregating in sheltered corners
glowing embers from another age.

some arbours that are still populated,
flitter with great flocks of gold
tethered, but soon to flight

behind the public park rails
wet barked trunks of maples
stand twisted between western
winds and seductive suns;
glistening shields of iron
ranked and filed
against the winter ruling

there is no room now for ornament
nor leaf
life held tight in shielded candle-buds
while fallen comrades lie freely
soon to resume their sidereal trip.

Ode

To a

Bottle of

Red Wine

Purple swollen grape

Speaks of love's bruised

lips, –   Old blood in an

ancient mating. Memories

opine, of a twisted vine

In   earthen pots, waiting.

Prometheus Bound

The furnace roar of the morning traffic
burns up my dreams
and I return to daylight
and the toils of man
bound
by no greater weight
than the banal.

Moon

By the sea's shore I stand
wild eyed
heart laid bare in open chest,
and the sinking full-faced moon
draws me
and thee
relentlessly to it's lonely bosom.

The Fire

Sun filled days of delusion times
mock me now
and leave no room for unhappiness

a few dreams tipped out
libation of the gods
lets the now come flooding in

I sit in front of fire
release of summer's sun
and beat of birds' wing undone

memories in branches now felled and
heaped upon the grate of past
present before future cast.

Sleeping Woman

after Toulouse Lautrec

Cheeks still bruised by sleep,
a single eyelid
rebounds,
and spies last night's lover
pen poised,
taking an image
not willingly given.

Beside her
where he has lain, is now cold,
but where they came together
is indelibly marked in knotted sheets
and tangled mind.

Who is this man
who now coldly sketches
a body that just hours before
led him to total surrender?

Budapest

Here in Budapest
the dawn of a nation-earth
seems now to be a distinct possibility.

The stuka pigeons have been banished
from the black-bladed roofs;
confined to iron rails
on the prickly, shingled shores
of the sleeping Buda,
and its Danubian companion.

Here is a river so confident
in its own importance, it
flows east, not west,
or north, or south;
rolling with the earth's turn,
it makes its own dark sea.

On the bank, empty fossilised shoes,
forlorn, speak with tongues of brass,
where Chinese tourists now gather
their shoes filled to over-flowing,
and pointing a way forward,
as they progress in digital frames,
 past the newly planted memory trees
 ... Ginko biloba ...
memories of Hiroshima
imprinted on their genes.

Angela Cox

Emily

She came to me,
cocooned and unwarned,
thinking she was safe in a world
she held tight about her,
as an old crone holds her shawl
against a bullying wind.

Our worlds collide,
and she is shocked by my strong
and cutting words
Walls crumble in confusion
and tears well up.

I glimpse a child
still hiding.

She told me I was hurtful, and I agreed,
my tool of last resort being hurt
against the bitter way she strewed
white rose petals of disdain,
each and every one
with the blood-red mark of pain.

And then she asked my name.
to know who it was that dare intrude on her
and when I spoke again,
she released her child name into my care
—like a butterfly—
and almost smiled.

Jeremiah B

His philosophical arguments
no longer allow me any new hypotheses
he is fixed in a pastiche of memories and
returning images, sparked randomly
from the flint walls that surround.
a little more understanding, possibly,
though now I am the age he was,
the Elder he will always be.

his first passing was sad but accepted
his final passing, through me
now looms, and will largely go unnoticed;
a world extinguished by
the death of a memory

neither monument, nor tombstone, nor plaque
can contain his spirit, and
just a few blackened words,
— Hiroshima moment of passing —
are left behind, as a burnt after-image,
on this page.

Remembering

Shocked awake
by the clarity of my vision
I struggle

to keep the walls
I have built
stone by heartfelt stone

crumbling
before the crush of
Presence

suspense of half-wake world
holds my mother's young face
separated from a wedding photograph

by intent and desire
hair frozen in the only perm
that lasted longer than a week
- she joked,

then embrace of memory
outs a lurking tear
and cold clay recaps.

Roots

I came bearing sheets of forked ideas
and web-linked names of strangers
from whose loins I'd sprung.
I came as a city dweller,
to find in what small and mean house, or field,
my predecessors had struggled, unaware as yet
that more could be known
than the next harvest, the next child.

At first I found three modern houses,
complete with double garages, new cars,
and trampolines; each fresh house
with an apron of closely manicured useless grass,
whose clippings, heaped to rot, led me up the lane way
to where the ditch was still a'growing,
and the years were taken back
to when the moss covered stones,
were still naked in their busyness,
and when a bend was first turned
    . . . for God knows what reason.

It is to this bend I go now
this willful or unconscious hieroglyph,
where one man stopped
and made our family's home.

I find the first weathered and decaying house,
single storied, single roomed, one eyed and open mouthed,
silent in its memories of house proud ornament
busy courtesan hens, and other 'yard to pots.'
At the second house, a horse waited, half door open
and I was recognised
as one of those who braided straw to bend its will
and so, it tipped its head and snorted.
We gazed, exchanging memories, and

I saw in his stead, Maureen and Delia;
mother and farmer's daughter,
names I know from a census night,
that were impressed by pen, clumsy in thickened hand
listing proudly read and write:
English for the future,
English and Irish, for the past.

Three cottages in all, with no door facing another
so each man, father and son,
could leave in the morning and go his own way.
From here, at the age of fifteen, my great-grandfather,
had left and crossed the fields to another farm
picked by the same calculation and observation
he learned at the side of a towering leg,
that was never uncovered, never revealed as flesh.

Even in death, those trunks had remained so,
covered by a shroud
that strangely stretched from chin to toe,
and those great hands that had spread seed
were now knuckled, and bound,
restrained by prayer, and rosary bead.

In the graveyard of Kilcolman where he lies now,
within a worms length of farmers
who once eyed his land with intent
between the lichen and the moss,
I search in vain for a carved name,
that would tell me, I too lie here in part.

And the western wind
that is without beginning or end
fills all the empty spaces between them
and me, and around these stone placements
I stagger, not knowing where, and when,
I am to fall.
continued . . .

Suddenly, from the derelict church, of rounded stone and sky,
a shivering dog fox bolts from where the hunters lie,
and I am shocked to see, as if it was always there,
a landscape shared with toil and care,
and a rough hewn cart, followed by a skipping waif,
and a tired, stooped man, with chin on forearm
on upright spade, gazes wistfully in my direction,
and sees his future, before him laid.

Snow Girl

There was George, and Dave, and me
all indentured and marked by trade
three old lions without a carnivorous tooth
between us that had not been worn down
by age and grinding dreams,
three redundant worker bees
now volunteering to support
a commune's dream in a city garden.

The snow-lashes had fallen overnight
one to another in their thousands bound,
wedded together into one white promise
they were a bride's promise,
a child's playground.

We old men, job weary with work
and wanting to play, dug deep
and heaped a man of snow
discarded scarecrow hat on top
and Ashling added the buttons
and ornament,
as children and women are inclined to do.

Oh Ashling the young, Ashling the bright
Ashling with the one
with the perfect white teeth.

It was George who first forgot his senior status
gathered two snowballs from the ground;
gloving them into battle ready shape.

.
Oh Ashling the young, Ashling the bright
Ashling with the one
with the perfect white teeth.

Then, on realising his age
and the solemnity of our present slowing state,
he paused and allowed his hands to curl
redundant, shame-filled, by his side.
I think it was the lack of twinkle in my eye
that finally signaled the passing of his fighting days,
and being a poet and a wag,
George mimed the careful weighing of each ball;
one final, testicular, comment on our state.

After a round of teenage shuffling,
and competition for comment most apt
Ashling saw the ancient loins had stirred,
and offered to take those now redundant balls
which George passed over; reluctantly disarmed
de-clawed.

She took them to where our snow man stood
and carefully placed her gifts upon his chest
and after two further button ornaments were pressed
she stood back with pride
to admire the snow girl by her side.

I knew then
that what was once a feverish fire,
could not now melt a snow girl . . .
my sole desire.

Caoimhe Harris

The Banal

I twist from the wrinkled embrace of sheets
and allow my feet to touch
gravity settles me.
Muscle, sinew and bone protest at their return
to the evolved upright state
The time for fruitful hiding
is past.

Pull back the curtains in confirmation
not anticipation,
the world has not ended, and if it had
how could I face it without clothes?
The stranger that allowed me to lose some moments,
lies half asleep in the darkened room
dream trodden eyes await a touch of endearment
or even recognition,
anything to lessen the isolation.

The action, once conceived is past,
and the pulling on of trousers
becomes the brutal erasure
of last night's shared passion.
I hobble self consciously from the room.

Now is the time to relish the first hot cup of tea
infusing its ragged tannins with blue-to-grey
smoke of cigarette;
before the tarry stub has quenched,
I light another one from its remains
and toss the empty packet in the bin,
finally severing all ties with the night before.

continued

Downstairs, the customers come and go,
and I brace myself against their relentless flow,
as I descend, and pass
from need, to others-need
. . . no space between.

The Homecoming

Down into the valley we drove
down to where the waters still roared;
the weight of surge
throwing itself hypnotically
over the weir, brief dance, then on again
never a backward glance.

Down from the fairy mountain:
a stream through the rushey glen,
down from where the banshees cry
past hawthorns twisted,
drops of blood for Christmas wren.

Down through the famine fields of stone
down from where the rag tree stands,
down from where each rock that leaves
the settling pile, takes with it
the memory of a placing hand.

Down into the valley we drove
down past graveyards of yore
down to where the river's roar
and mind's eye become one,
time's passage finally undone.

P. J. Bermingham

Ageing solar flares,
rusting dark bullet holes
in a chamber piss pot
that is an alzhiemers riddled brain.

This mourning
washing hands and face
fresh spring water memories
mixed with taste of toilet bowl.

In my father's wallet, there is a picture;
28 year old hurler
bow-tensed to strike
flying head of blonde hair
Hermes' wings; New York 1962.

I asked, "Do you know who that is?'
"Lovely, lovely,"— the fading, farewell reply.

Important Historical Events

A newspaper headline
in the largest font available
was my first lesson
on how to recognise an historical event.

Then the black and white flicker,
of a man on the moon,
a fallen president,
a speech of a dream.

Embedded we crawled
the word-shingled beach,
watched fireworks displayed
for bloodied civilians dismayed.

Tyrants everywhere were shown
the soles of our shoes
the wrath of our righteousness,
the judgment of our News.

A wall is chipped, a princess killed,
a president signs with twenty gifting pens,
and two towers are folded down
into the ground,
a child is born and a woman says no
. . . and expects it so.

As for important historical events . . .
a farmer in Colombia receives a text
on the price of coffee
and has time to tell stories,
that allow his children to dream
and a bee dips into a flower,
so the last seed
can be born.

Snow

The water of life is stilled
and I watch
as in slow motion
the falling eyelashes of snow
whisper me towards sleep
each and every fractal variation
yet unstained
by hormonal recreation

life is the messy one
from orifices that weep
and secrete, and defecate,
weaved between soiled and tangled sheets
in oyster stains drawn by semen filled sacks
we find little deaths:
preambles in the dark.

all men and beasts
and sentient things
fear death's embrace
whether it comes gently
or without warning
because death reorganizes
recycles
base elements once more
in concert.

Trees

Old planted trees
lift up the memory of bended back
and distant mind
hold high in mirrored branches
the swirling hopes and dreams
of those who sowed
and did not need to reap.

I trace my fingers
on the messaged bark
in search of thoughts
etched carefully there
by passing winds
and swaying sun
and find this shy message
exposed for all to see

Remember me
where stands this tree.

Elida Maiques

75

The Final Concert

I want to play in a band with a crazy name,
hear the base trombone that the blue whales blow,
trumpet with the elephant, and grunt with the lion,
hear the swarm and the hive, sing and jive.

I want to play in a band with a crazy name,
see the colours and the sounds, rise and fall,
a pulsing rainbow from life's one aura,
where my voice will not signal, fear to them all.

I want to play in a band with a crazy name,
be announced by the brassy Whooping Crane,
rhythms ratcheted up by Puerto Rican Crested Toads,
in the back, Cascade Frogs clearing their throats in vain.

I want to play in a band with a crazy name
Pacific Walrus plaintiff strumming;
wind section of Bare Shanked Screeching Owls,
and American Alligators, percussion rolling.

I want to play in a band with a crazy name,
where the Common Loon will make mocking fun,
of the all too serious Mexican grey wolf,
and the Polar Bear can still swallow the sun.

I want to play in a band with a crazy name,
a band that needs no more rehearsals,
a band that calls us all together,
a band with a crazy name like . . . Earth.

All the members of this band are on the current endangered species
list, and their song can be heard at rareearthtones.org
I would argue that man should also be now included on the list